LUTON LIBRARIES

D0182637

First published in the UK in 2014 by

Ivy Press

210 High Street

Lewes

East Sussex BN7 2NS

United Kingdom

www.ivypress.co.uk

ISBN: 978-1-78240-109-4

This book was conceived, designed and produced by

Ivy Press

CREATIVE DIRECTOR   Peter Bridgewater

PUBLISHER   Susan Kelly

COMMISSIONING EDITOR   Hazel Songhurst

MANAGING EDITOR   Hazel Songhurst

PROJECT EDITOR   Cath Senker

ART DIRECTOR   Kim Hankinson

DESIGNER   Kevin Knight

ILLUSTRATORS

Melvyn Evans (colour)

Marta Munoz (black and white)

Printed in China

Colour origination by Ivy Press Reprographics

10 9 8 7 6 5 4 3 2 1

EARTH
IN 30 SECONDS

ANITA GANERI

CONSULTANT: DR CHERITH MOSES

Ivy Kids

Contents

Amazing Earth
...in 60 seconds

Planet Earth is amazing. It's just a tiny speck in the vastness of the Universe but it is the only planet we know of that supports life. Its age is mind-boggling – around 5 billion years old. Yet new land can still form when volcanoes erupt. It is so huge that it would take you around 24 years to dig a hole to the other side. It is home to millions of different life-forms, some of them so tiny that you need a microscope to see them.

This book looks at fascinating topics about Earth, from our place in space to the importance of protecting our planet for the future.

From icy Poles to dry deserts, and from sky-high mountains to undersea landscapes, it shows you the natural wonders and drama of our restless planet, from wild weather to explosive volcanoes.

Each topic has a page to read as fast as you like, to grasp the main facts quickly. There's also a speedy sum-up, to give you the basics in a nutshell. Then you can turn Earth detective and try out the missions you'll find throughout. They will give you the chance to discover more about how your planet works. See for yourself why we have day and night, find out how mountains form, create a mini tornado in a bottle, and more.

Earth in space

The Universe is made up of millions and millions of galaxies, each travelling through space at incredible speed. Each one is made up of millions of stars. In one galaxy named the Milky Way, eight planets travel around a star, called the Sun. The third planet from the Sun is the Earth. In this chapter, you can read about the Earth's place in space and how the way that it moves causes day and night, and the seasons.

Earth in space
Glossary

axis An imaginary line through the centre of the Earth, around which it turns.

Equator An imaginary line around the Earth at an equal distance from the North and South Poles.

galaxy Any of the large systems of stars, planets and other objects in space – our galaxy is the Milky Way.

Milky Way The name of our galaxy, a large system of stars, planets and other objects in space.

Northern Hemisphere The half of the Earth north of the Equator.

orbit A curved path followed by a planet or an object as it moves around another object in space, such as a planet, star or moon.

planet A large ball-shaped object in space that moves around a star (such as the Sun) and receives light from it.

Poles The two points at the opposite ends of the Earth's axis.

Solar System The Sun and all the planets that move around it.

Southern Hemisphere The half of the Earth south of the Equator.

Universe The whole of space and everything in it, including the Earth, the planets and the stars.

Place in space

...in 30 seconds

Planet Earth is one of eight planets that orbit the Sun in space. Together with Mercury, Venus, Mars, Jupiter, Saturn, Uranus and Neptune, the Sun and Earth make up our Solar System. Our Solar System is a minute part of the vast Universe, which is made up of everything that exists. It's hard to imagine!

Earth and the other planets travel around the Sun in oval-shaped paths, called orbits. The Earth lies an average of 149,597,871 km (92,955,807 miles) away from the Sun. It takes the Earth around 365 days to orbit the Sun.

Scientists believe that the whole of the Solar System was formed from part of a vast cloud of gas and dust nearly 5 billion years ago. As far as we know, Earth is the only place in the Universe that can support life. But who knows?

3-second sum-up

The Earth is one of eight planets that orbit the Sun.

3-minute mission Size up the solar system

You need: • Paper sheet 1 m x 1 m (40 x 40 inches) • 55 cm (22 inches) of string • Pencil • Sticky tape • Scissors • Ruler • Different-sized sticker circles, and coins, counters or lids to draw around for the planets • Extra paper

1 To draw the Sun, tie the string to a pencil, leaving 50 cm (20 inches) loose. Tape the string end to the centre of the large paper sheet. Pull the string taut and draw a circle.
2 Roughly match your stickers and circular objects to the planet diameters. Use them to complete your paper solar system.

DIAMETERS:
Sun 1 m
Mercury 0.4 cm
Venus 0.9 cm
Earth 0.9 cm
Mars 0.5 cm
Jupiter 10 cm
Saturn 8 cm
Uranus 3.6 cm
Neptune 3.5 cm

Earth is one of 8 planets in the solar system. It is the third planet from the Sun.

Neptune

Uranus

From space, Earth looks blue because two-thirds of its surface is covered in water.

Earth's year is 365 days long – the time it takes it to orbit the Sun.

Earth's orbit

The length of Earth's orbit is 939.9 million km (584 million miles).

Mercury

Venus

Sun

Saturn

Moon

Earth

Mars

Jupiter

The Sun is huge compared to Earth. 109 Earths side by side would match the Sun's diameter!

Spinning Earth
...in 30 seconds

We're on the move! The Earth beneath your feet is spinning very slowly on its axis, an imaginary line running through the middle from the North Pole to the South Pole.

The Earth spins all the time but you do not feel any movement because it turns smoothly and at a steady speed.

It takes 23 hours, 56 minutes and 4 seconds for the Earth to spin around once on its axis. During that time, every place turns towards the Sun and has daytime. Then it turns away from the Sun and has night-time. When it is daytime on one side of the Earth, it is night-time on the other. When you are getting up for breakfast, people on the other side of the world are getting ready for bed!

During the day, it looks as if the Sun moves across the sky. In fact, it does not move at all. It is the Earth that is moving. The Earth always spins in the same direction, towards the east. So you see the Sun rising in the east and setting in the west every day.

3-second sum-up

The Earth spins on its axis, giving us day and night.

3-minute mission Spinning Earth

To see how we get day and night, find a football to be the Earth and a torch for the Sun. Tape outlines of the continents on the ball. Close the curtains. Turn the ball and ask a friend to shine the torch on it. You will see the outlines on the ball move into the light, then into the darkness.

The Earth spins around on its axis but the Sun remains still.

The Sun does not move.

This side of the Earth is facing away from the Sun. It is night-time.

North Pole

The Earth is turning on its axis.

South Pole

This side of the Earth is facing the Sun. It is daytime.

Changing seasons
...in 30 seconds

Did you know that the Earth leans to one side? The Earth is tilted on its axis at an angle of 23.5 degrees. As it orbits the Sun, different places receive different amounts of light and heat throughout the year. This causes the seasons.

When the North Pole tilts towards the Sun, it is summer in the Northern Hemisphere. The weather is warm and the days are long. Meanwhile, it is winter in the Southern Hemisphere. The weather is cold and the days are short.

When the South Pole tilts towards the Sun, the seasons are the other way around. It is winter in the Northern Hemisphere and summer in the Southern Hemisphere. In between summer and winter, places that lie between the Equator and the Poles have spring and autumn. Each season lasts for about three months.

Places at the Equator are not affected by the Earth's tilt. They always lean towards the Sun and are hot all year round. The year is divided into wet and dry times. At the Poles, there are two seasons – six months of winter and six months of summer.

3-second sum-up

Seasons happen because the Earth is tilted on its axis.

3-minute mission Show the seasons

Hold up a globe – or a ball marked with the North and South Poles. Ask a friend to hold a beach ball to be the Sun. Tilt your globe and walk slowly around the Sun. Stop when you think it is summer in the Northern Hemisphere. Are you right? Look at the illustration on the opposite page to check.

The seasons happen because
different parts of the Earth face
towards and away from the
Sun during its orbit.

The Earth is tilted
on its axis as it
orbits the Sun.

The North Pole tilts
towards the Sun.
It is summer in the
Northern Hemisphere.

The North Pole tilts
away from the Sun.
It is winter in the
Northern Hemisphere.

N

S

N

S

It is winter
in the Southern
Hemisphere.

It is summer
in the Southern
Hemisphere.

Earth's structure

When you go for a walk, do you ever stop to think what is going on beneath your feet? What is our planet actually made from? The ground you walk on is hard rock but it doesn't always stay firmly in one place. Over millions of years, it has cracked and shifted, creating the continents and mountains we have today, and causing dramatic earthquakes and volcanoes. In this chapter, you can read more about the restless Earth.

Earth's structure
Glossary

block mountain A mountain formed when cracks in the Earth's crust force enormous blocks of rock upwards.

continent One of the large land masses of the Earth, such as Europe, Asia or Africa.

continental drift The slow movement of the continents towards and away from each other.

core The innermost part of the Earth.

crust The outer layer of the Earth – the ground we walk on.

dome mountain A mountain formed when magma under the ground pushes the rocks above into a round bulge.

erode To gradually destroy and remove the surface of something through the action of wind, rain or other natural agents.

fold mountain A mountain formed when two tectonic plates crash together; the rocks crumple upwards into gigantic folds.

igneous rock Rock formed when magma (melted or liquid material below the Earth's surface) turns solid, especially after it has poured out of a volcano.

lava Hot liquid rock that comes out of a volcano on to the Earth's surface.

magma Very hot liquid rock found below the Earth's surface.

mantle The part of the Earth below the crust and surrounding the core.

metamorphic rock Rock formed by the action of heat or pressure.

sedimentary rock Rock formed from the sand, stones, mud, etc, that settle at the bottom of lakes.

shock wave A movement of very high air pressure that is caused by an earthquake.

sphere Any object that is completely round, for example, a ball.

tectonic plate One of the huge sheets of rock that form the Earth's surface.

Crust to core

...in 30 seconds

The Earth is not perfectly round. It is a squashed sphere, which is flatter at the top and bottom. The Earth bulges out around the middle, at the Equator. The solid, rocky ground you walk on is the Earth's crust.

The crust varies in thickness. Under the continents, it is an average of 35 km (21 miles) thick but only 6–10 km (4–6 miles) thick under the oceans.

Beneath the crust is a layer of rock called the mantle. Just under the crust, the mantle is so hot that some of it has melted to make soft, molten rock, called magma.

Under the mantle is the Earth's core. It has two layers: the outer and inner core. The outer core is liquid metal, mostly iron and nickel. The inner core is solid metal, with a super-hot temperature of up to 4,500°C (8,100°F)! But it does not melt because it is pressed hard by the weight of the layers all around it.

3-second sum-up

The Earth is made of different layers, from the crust to the core.

The centre of the Earth

The distance from the crust to the centre of the Earth is about 6,400 km (4,000 miles). If it was possible, it would take you 53 days to walk there without stopping! So far, the deepest hole ever drilled by humans only reached around 12 km (7 miles) down.

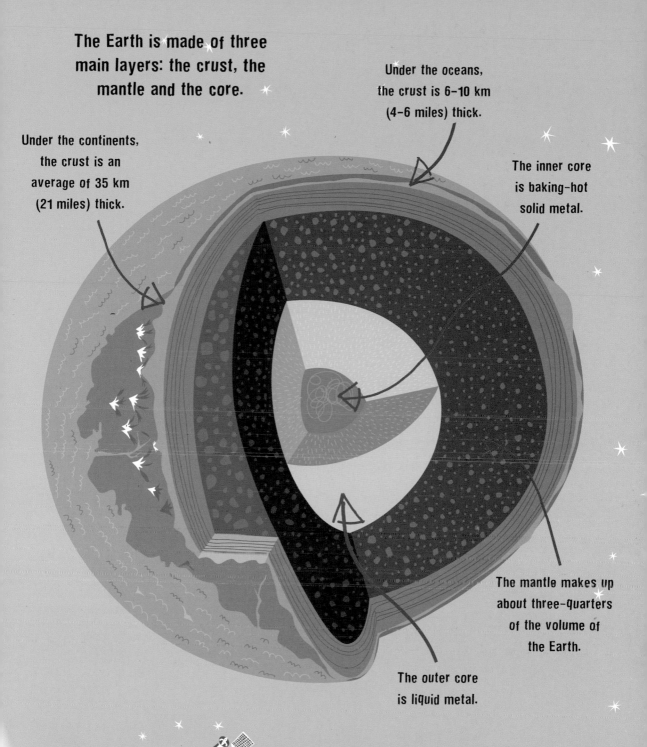

The Earth is made of three main layers: the crust, the mantle and the core.

Under the oceans, the crust is 6–10 km (4–6 miles) thick.

Under the continents, the crust is an average of 35 km (21 miles) thick.

The inner core is baking-hot solid metal.

The mantle makes up about three-quarters of the volume of the Earth.

The outer core is liquid metal.

Drifting continents

...in 30 seconds

The continents are moving! The crust of the Earth is cracked into giant pieces, called tectonic plates. There are seven large plates and many smaller ones. The plates move a few centimetres every year, carrying the continents with them. This movement is known as continental drift. The plates drift on the layer of molten magma, beneath, in the Earth's mantle.

In some places, the edges of the plates move apart. In other places, they slide past each other. Sometimes, the edges of two plates collide. These movements cause earthquakes and volcanoes, and build mountains.

Continental drift has been happening for millions of years. About 250 million years ago, all of today's continents were joined together in one super-continent, called Pangaea. Pangaea later separated into Laurasia and Gondwanaland. Gondwanaland then split to form Antarctica, South America, Africa, India, and parts of South-East Asia and Australia. Laurasia divided to make North America, Europe and Asia.

3-second sum-up

The Earth's crust is cracked into pieces, which drift slowly.

3-minute mission Porridge plate tectonics

Ask an adult to help you cook some porridge. When it's just been cooked, it is hot and liquid, like the magma of the Earth. Allow the porridge to cool a little – the surface forms a cool skin, like the Earth's crust. If you reheat it, the surface will move, and bubbles appear through the 'crust', like volcanoes erupting.

Earth's continents drift on seven tectonic plates. Over millions of years the continents have moved to where they are today.

250,000,000 years ago

There was just one super-continent, called Pangaea.

Pangaea broke into Laurasia and Gondwanaland.

200,000,000 years ago

Gondwanaland split into Africa and South America. Laurasia then split into North America, Europe and Asia.

65,000,000 years ago

Today

Today there are seven continents.

Rocks and minerals

...in 30 seconds

If you dig down into the ground, you will come to solid rock. Rocks are the building blocks of the Earth's crust.

Rocks come in all kinds of shapes, textures and colours. There are three types.

Igneous rocks start as red-hot magma deep inside the Earth. The magma rises towards the surface where it may erupt from a volcano. It cools and hardens to form igneous rocks, such as basalt, granite and obsidian.

Sedimentary rocks are made from little fragments of rock, sand and mud that have been eroded, and the remains of tiny sea animals. Over millions of years, they are compressed (squashed tightly together) into layers of rock, like sandstone, limestone and chalk.

Metamorphic rocks are igneous or sedimentary rocks that are changed by heat deep underground, or by the huge forces that push up mountains. They include marble, slate and quartzite.

3-second sum-up

The Earth's crust is made up of different rocks and minerals.

3-minute mission How rocks are made

Pressure and heat act to make rocks – see how this works!

You need: • 3 slices each of white and wholemeal bread • Greaseproof paper • Heavy books • Microwave • Adult helper

1 Stack the bread, alternating white and wholemeal slices. Wrap in greaseproof paper.

2 Place books on the stack to squash it. Then remove the books.

3 Place the bread in the microwave for 1 minute. The heat and pressure make the bread hard – just how rocks are formed.

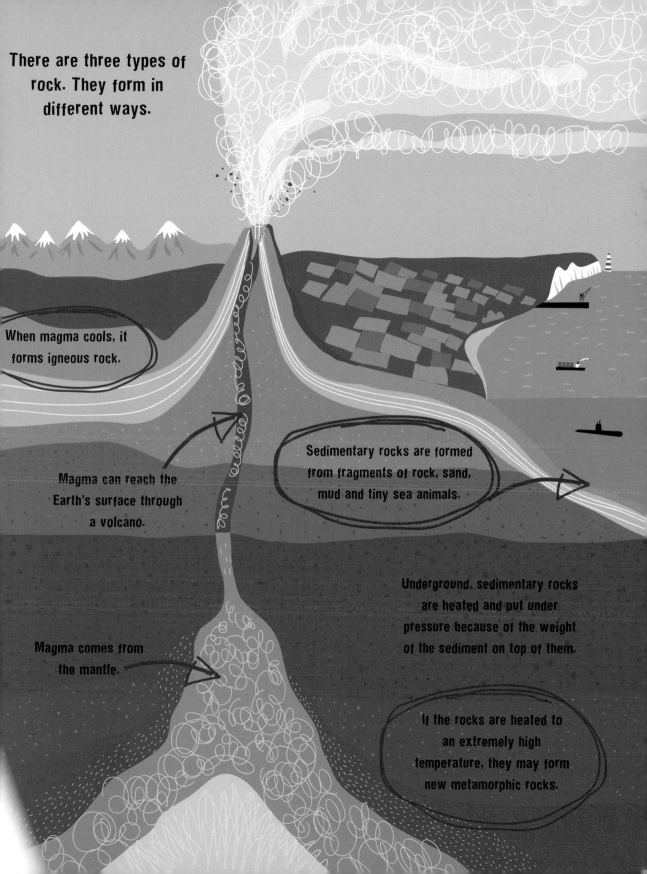

There are three types of rock. They form in different ways.

When magma cools, it forms igneous rock.

Magma can reach the Earth's surface through a volcano.

Magma comes from the mantle.

Sedimentary rocks are formed from fragments of rock, sand, mud and tiny sea animals.

Underground, sedimentary rocks are heated and put under pressure because of the weight of the sediment on top of them.

If the rocks are heated to an extremely high temperature, they may form new metamorphic rocks.

Volcanoes
...in 30 seconds

Volcanoes happen when magma and gases from deep inside the Earth are put under pressure and force their way to the surface through cracks in the crust. The magma may erupt as streams of red-hot rock or explode in clouds of ash and dust.

There are around 1,500 active volcanoes around the world. Most are located at the edges of the Earth's plates.

When magma reaches the Earth's surface, it is called lava. It can reach temperatures of 1,200°C (over 2,000°F) and flow at speeds of up to 100 km (60 miles) per hour.

Think of a volcano and you probably imagine a cone-shaped mountain. But not all volcanoes are like that. Their shape depends on how thick the lava is and how violently they erupt. Thick, sticky lava builds tall, steep-sided cones. Thin, runny lava builds gently sloping, dome-shaped volcanoes.

3-second sum-up

Volcanoes erupt when magma forces its way to the surface.

Volcanologists

Volcanologists study volcanoes as a job. It's an exciting, challenging and sometimes dangerous career. Some volcanologists study active volcanoes to try to work out how to protect the people nearby. They may find themselves close to a volcano when it erupts. They'll sense the ground-shaking eruption, hear the loud noises of explosions and breaking rocks and may even feel some ash pouring down on them. To become a volcanologist, you need to study the sciences, maths and computing.

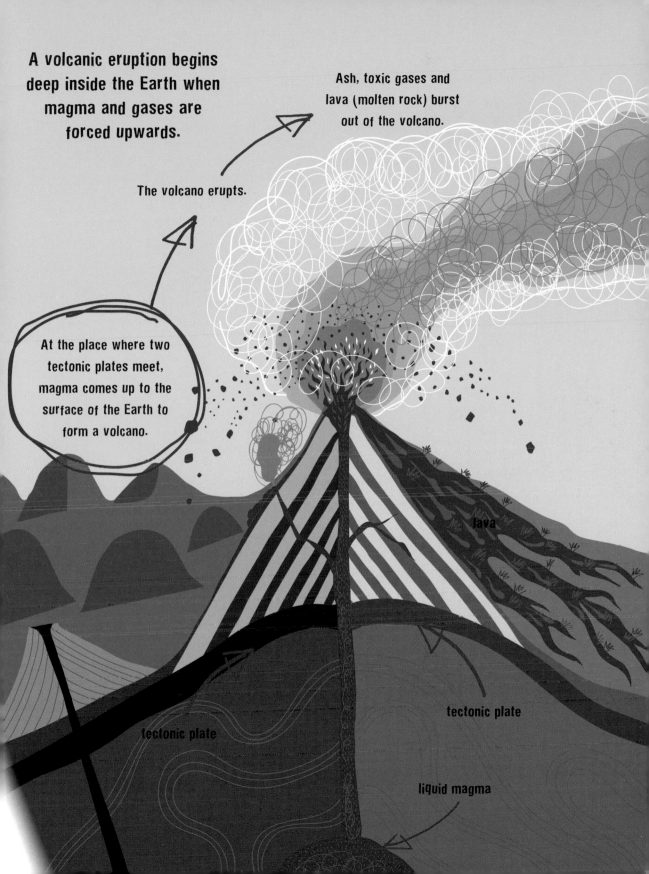

A volcanic eruption begins deep inside the Earth when magma and gases are forced upwards.

Ash, toxic gases and lava (molten rock) burst out of the volcano.

The volcano erupts.

At the place where two tectonic plates meet, magma comes up to the surface of the Earth to form a volcano.

lava

tectonic plate

tectonic plate

liquid magma

Earthquakes

...in 30 seconds

Sometimes the edges of tectonic plates get stuck. But the plates keep moving. They push against each other. Pressure builds up under the ground. Suddenly, the pressure is released. The rocks slip, sending out gigantic shock waves.

The ground shakes violently. It's an earthquake! The shock waves from a massive earthquake can travel thousands of kilometres around the Earth. Buildings can tumble down, cars crash, power lines fall, and people may be killed or injured.

Seismologists (earthquake experts) mostly use the Richter scale to measure earthquakes. It grades earthquakes from 0–10, according to their magnitude – the amount of energy released when the rocks break. Each step up the scale means a 30-fold increase in energy. A magnitude 4 quake on the Richter scale is a whopping 900 times more powerful than a level 2 earthquake.

3-second sum-up

An earthquake happens when the Earth's plates move suddenly.

3-minute mission Shock waves

To see how shock waves work, simply throw a pebble in a pond. Watch the waves ripple outwards. They are largest where they form, and gradually get smaller as they move away.

Go to this website to see some animations that show how earthquakes happen: http://earthquake.usgs.gov/learn/animations/

Earthquakes can be devasting! The sudden movement of the plates causes huge shock waves.

This cross-section shows the plates moving – but the edges are stuck.

The rocks suddenly slip. The earthquake waves begin here, at the focus.

The earthquake waves reach the surface at the epicentre, directly above the focus.

The earthquake waves shake the ground.

Mountains

...in 30 seconds

Movements of the Earth's crust have created most of the world's great mountains. When two plates crash together, the rocks crumple upwards into gigantic folds – and make fold mountains. The Himalaya mountains in Asia formed like this 40 million years ago.

When faults or cracks in the Earth's crust force enormous blocks of rock upwards, block mountains form. They have flatter tops than fold mountains. The Sierra Nevada range in North America is formed of block mountains.

Magma under the ground can push upwards to build dome mountains. The magma pushes the rocks above into a round bulge. It cools to form solid rock. The Black Hills in North America formed in this way. Volcanoes can erupt and create mountains too. Mount Kilimanjaro in Tanzania and Mount Etna in Italy formed like this.

Did you know that mountain ranges can stretch for thousands of kilometres? The longest mountain range on Earth is the Andes in South America. It's around 7,250 km (4,500 miles) long.

3-second sum-up

The Earth's crust can shift to create massive mountains.

3-minute mission Mountain making

Make your own fold mountains.

You need: • 4 strips of different-coloured modelling clay • 2 wooden blocks

1 Arrange the strips, one on top of the other, like layers of rock.

2 Put a wooden block at each end, to be the plates.

3 Push the blocks towards each other, as if the plates are colliding.

4 The harder you push, the more crumpled the layers will be.

The Himalaya mountains were formed by movements of the Earth's crust.

The tectonic plate carrying India crashed into the plate carrying the rest of Asia.

The Himalaya mountains started to form.

Indian plate

Asian plate

The two plates pushed against each other, and the Earth's crust was squeezed upwards.

They became the highest mountains on Earth – and they are still growing!

Weather and climate

What is the weather like where you are? The weather happens in the Earth's atmosphere, as the Sun's rays warm the air. It happens every day, all of the time. Climate is the pattern of weather in a place over a long period of time, from cold and icy at the Poles to hot and steamy in the tropics. In this chapter, you'll find out how the rain that drops on you has fallen many times before, and learn about some of the wildest winds on the planet.

Weather and climate
Glossary

air current The movement of air in a particular direction.

air pressure The force of the air in the atmosphere pressing down on the Earth's surface.

alto cloud Middle-level cloud.

atmosphere The mixture of gases that surrounds the Earth.

charge (electrical) The amount of electricity that is carried by a substance.

cirrus cloud A type of light cloud that forms high in the sky.

climate The regular pattern of weather conditions of a particular place.

condense To change from a gas into a liquid, for example, when water vapour turns into water.

cumulus cloud A type of thick white cloud that forms low in the sky.

cumulonimbus cloud A high mass of thick cloud with a flat base, often seen during thunderstorms.

debris During a tornado, pieces of wood, metal, brick or rubbish that are carried away by the strong winds.

evaporate When a liquid evaporates, it changes into a gas, for example, water turns into steam.

exosphere The region near the outer edge of a planet's atmosphere.

eye (of storm) A calm area at the centre of a storm.

mesosphere The part of the Earth's atmosphere which is between 50 and 85 km (31 to 53 miles) from the ground, between the stratosphere and the thermosphere.

microclimate The weather in a particular small area, especially when this is different from the weather in the surrounding area.

polar Connected with, or near to the North or South Pole.

storm surge An unusual rise in the level of the ocean near the coast, caused by wind from a severe storm.

stratosphere The layer of the Earth's atmosphere between about 16 and 50 km (10 to 31 miles) above the surface of the Earth.

stratus cloud A type of cloud that forms low in the sky, making a grey layer covering the sky.

supercell An extremely powerful thunderstorm.

temperate Having mild temperatures, never very hot or very cold.

thermosphere The region of the atmosphere above the mesosphere, from 85 to 500 km (53 to about 300 miles) above the Earth.

tropical Relating to the tropics, the area just above and below the Equator. The climate is warm or hot, and moist all year round.

troposphere The lowest layer of the Earth's atmosphere, between the surface of the Earth and about 8 to 16 km (about 5 to 10 miles) above the surface.

vortex A mass of air in a tornado that spins around very fast and pulls things into its centre.

water vapour A mass of very small drops of water in the air.

Earth's atmosphere
...in 30 seconds

So what's between us on Earth and black space beyond? Our Earth is surrounded by a giant blanket of gases, called the atmosphere. The atmosphere has different layers. We live in the troposphere. It reaches up to 8–16 km (5–10 miles) above the Earth's surface. The troposphere provides us with oxygen to breathe.

The air in the troposphere never stays still. It is constantly being moved about by changes in air pressure and temperature. The moving air helps to spread the Sun's heat around the world and causes our weather.

Feeling under pressure? The weight of the air in the atmosphere presses down on everything on the Earth, including you. This is air pressure. It varies all the time. Lows are areas of low pressure, with the lowest pressure in the centre. Highs are areas of high pressure, with the highest pressure in the centre. Lows usually bring wet, cloudy weather. Highs usually bring sunny, dry weather.

3-second sum-up

The atmosphere is a blanket of gases around the Earth.

3-minute mission Air-pressure trick

You need: • Piece of card 7.5 x 12.5 cm (3 x 5 inches) • A glass • Water

1 Fill the glass a third full with water.

2 Wet the lip of the glass and cover the top with the card. Hold the card in place.

3 Take the glass to the sink and turn it upside down. Carefully, take your hand away.

4 What happens? The force of air pressure against the card should hold the card in place.

The atmosphere is a blanket of gases that surrounds the Earth. It is made up of 5 layers.

Exosphere:
up to space,
10,000 km
(6,200 miles)

International Space Station
330 km (205 miles)

Thermosphere:
up to **500 km**
(about 300 miles)

Satellite
160 km (100 miles)

Mesosphere:
up to **85 km**
(53 miles)

Military jet aircraft
35 km (22 miles)

Thunderstorm cloud
13 km (8 miles)

Mount Everest
9 km (6 miles)

Stratosphere:
up to **50 km**
(31 miles)

Passenger aeroplane
13 km (8 miles)

Troposphere:
up to **8-16 km**
(5-10 miles)

Water cycle

...in 30 seconds

The water that soaks you when it rains is on a long journey. The sea is where the journey begins. Water evaporates from the sea to form water vapour in the atmosphere. You can't see water vapour, but when the air contains a lot, it feels warm and sticky.

If the water vapour cools, it condenses into tiny droplets of water, or tiny ice crystals. These droplets and crystals make up the clouds you see in the sky. If they grow large enough, they fall from the clouds as rain or snow. Rain and melted snow flow from the land into streams and rivers, which carry the water back to the sea.

Water is constantly moving between the seas, the atmosphere, the land, and rivers and lakes. This circulation of water is called the water cycle.

Clouds are part of the water cycle. Next time you're outside try to spot these types: cumulus – heaped, lumpy clouds; stratus – layered clouds; cumulonimbus – rain clouds; alto – middle-level clouds.

3-second sum-up

The water cycle is the circulation of water on Earth and in the atmosphere.

3-minute mission Making rain

You need: • Large glass bowl • Warm water • Kitchen foil or food wrap • Ice cubes

1 Pour warm water into the bowl until the water is about 5 cm (2 inches) deep.

2 Cut a piece of kitchen foil and use it to tightly cover the bowl.

3 Put some ice cubes on top of the foil.

4 Water evaporates from the bottom of the bowl to form water vapour. When the water vapour hits the cold foil it condenses, and 'rain' drips back into your 'sea'!

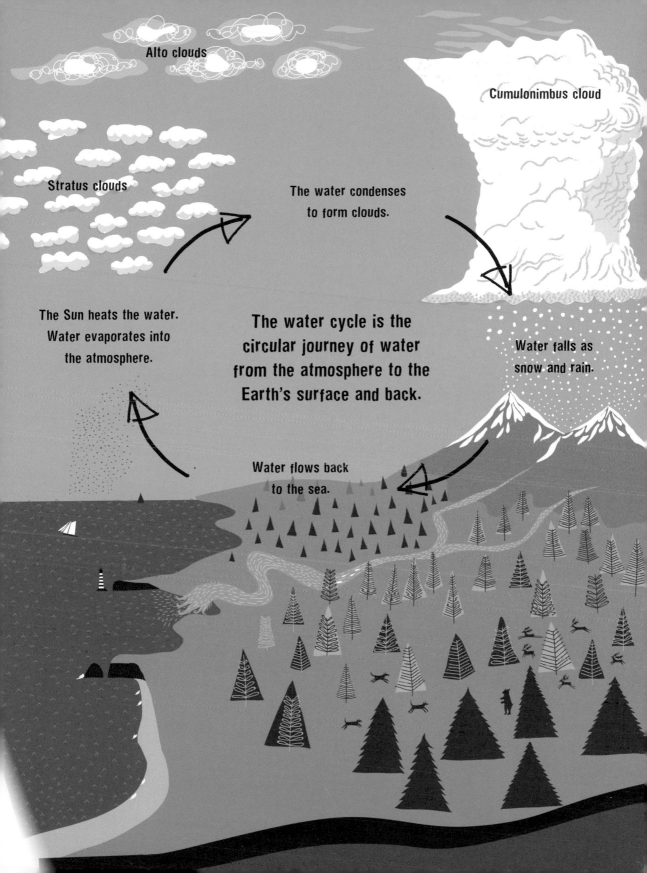

Alto clouds

Cumulonimbus cloud

Stratus clouds

The water condenses
to form clouds.

The Sun heats the water.
Water evaporates into
the atmosphere.

The water cycle is the
circular journey of water
from the atmosphere to the
Earth's surface and back.

Water falls as
snow and rain.

Water flows back
to the sea.

Thunder and lightning
...in 30 seconds

As you read this, about 2,000 thunderstorms are raging around the world. Crashes of thunder and lightning flashes are two of the Earth's most spectacular weather events.

Lightning is a super-powerful spark of electricity that jumps through the air. A bolt of lightning heats the air to thousands of degrees Celsius. This heat makes the air expand suddenly, which causes the rumbling boom of thunder.

Thunderstorms happen when cumulus clouds keep growing into towering storm clouds, called cumulonimbus clouds. These can be more than 10 km (6 miles) high! Powerful air currents flow up and down inside the clouds, building up huge electric charges. Positive charges grow in the top of the cloud and negative charges grow in the bottom.

When the charges grow large enough, electricity leaps from one part of a cloud to another, between clouds, or between a cloud and the ground. You see this as lightning. Sheet lightning is a bright flash inside a cloud; forked lightning is a bright streak.

3-minute mission Thunderstorm distance

Light travels much faster than sound, so you see lightning before you hear thunder. It's easy to work out how far away a thunderstorm is.

1 When you see lightning, start counting seconds on a stopwatch.

2 Stop counting when you hear the thunder.

3 Divide the number of seconds by 3 to work out the distance to the storm in kilometres (divide by 5 for miles). Sound travels 1 mile every 5 seconds and 1 km every 3 seconds. For example, if you count 6 seconds, the distance is 2 km.

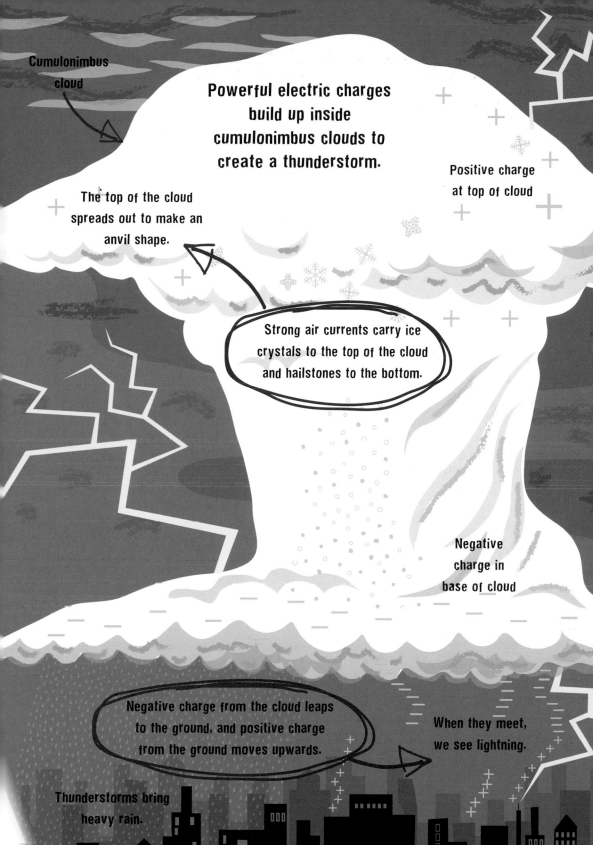

Cumulonimbus cloud

Powerful electric charges build up inside cumulonimbus clouds to create a thunderstorm.

Positive charge at top of cloud

The top of the cloud spreads out to make an anvil shape.

Strong air currents carry ice crystals to the top of the cloud and hailstones to the bottom.

Negative charge in base of cloud

Negative charge from the cloud leaps to the ground, and positive charge from the ground moves upwards.

When they meet, we see lightning.

Thunderstorms bring heavy rain.

Hurricanes

...in 30 seconds

Hurricanes are enormous spinning storms. They bring super-strong winds, torrential rain, towering waves at sea, and can cause flooding on land.

A hurricane starts as a group of thunderstorms that form over warm tropical seas near the Equator. Sometimes, the thunderstorms develop into a swirling storm, called a tropical storm. Some tropical storms die away, but some carry on growing, drawing energy from the warm sea they pass over. Their winds get stronger and stronger, and they grow into bands of towering clouds full of rain.

When the winds inside a tropical storm reach 118 km (73 miles) per hour, the storm is officially a hurricane. The Saffir-Simpson scale measures the strength of a hurricane, from category 1 to category 5. Category 5 hurricanes bring winds of more than 226 km (141 miles) per hour!

As a hurricane moves across the sea, it pushes up a bulge of water called a storm surge. If the hurricane reaches land, the water can sweep inland, causing flooding. In 2005, the storm surge of Hurricane Katrina badly flooded the US city of New Orleans. A hurricane's high winds and heavy rain also cause serious damage.

3-second sum-up

A hurricane is a huge swirling storm with very strong winds.

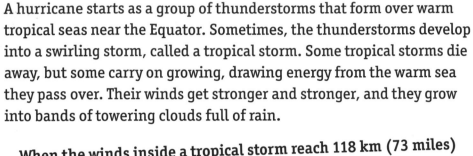

Naming hurricanes

All hurricanes are given names. The World Meteorological Organization makes up name lists, one for each year. The lists are reused every six years. If a hurricane causes a lot of damage, its name is never used again. Andrew, Mitch and Katrina are examples of retired names.

Hurricanes form over warm, tropical seas and cause terrible damage and flooding if they reach land.

The wall of cloud around the eye is called the eye wall.

The eye is a cloud-free hole in the centre.

Hurricanes spin anti-clockwise in the Northern Hemisphere. In the Southern Hemisphere they spin clockwise.

A hurricane brings strong winds, heavy rain and thunderstorms.

Tornadoes

...in 30 seconds

Did you know that the fiercest winds on Earth are found inside tornadoes? Tornadoes are twisting, whirling columns of air that bring winds of up to 480 km (300 miles) per hour. These are strong enough to smash buildings to pieces, toss cars around, and even pluck trains from their tracks.

Tornadoes are formed by extremely energetic thunderstorms, called supercells. Powerful air currents inside a supercell create a spinning column of air, called a vortex, at the base of the cell. A tornado happens when this column of air descends from the cell and touches the ground.

The air on the outside of a tornado spirals upwards, carrying debris with it. The fast-flying debris can be carried many kilometres before being dropped back to Earth, causing terrible damage. Tornadoes can measure more than 3 km (2 miles) across, and move across the ground at speeds of up to 115 km (71 miles) per hour.

3-second sum-up

A tornado is a spinning column of air with extremely powerful winds.

3-minute mission Tornado in a bottle

You need: • Large, clear glass jar with a lid • Washing-up liquid • Food colouring • Water

1 Fill the jar with water almost to the top.

2 Add a few drops of food colouring to the water, and a few drops of washing-up liquid.

3 Swirl the jar around and around to make the water spin round inside it, then stop.

4 Can you see the tornado-like shape inside the jar?

A tornado happens when the air currents inside a supercell thunderstorm form a vortex that touches the ground.

Vortex

Winds blow around the vortex.

The tornado moves across the ground.

Debris is picked up by the winds.

Climate zones
...in 30 seconds

What kinds of weather do you see in one year? Climate is the pattern of weather that happens in a place over a long period of time. It's not the same as the weather you have from day to day. If you live somewhere that has warm summers, you might get a few cold days in summer, but generally, the weather is warm.

Different parts of the world have different climates. These areas are called climate zones. There are three main climate zones – polar, tropical and temperate.

Places around the South Pole and the North Pole have a polar climate. It is cold all the time, with freezing-cold winters and no warm summers. Places near the Equator have a tropical climate. It is baking hot all year round, and there are dry and rainy times. Places between the Equator and the Poles have a temperate climate. There are four seasons, with a warm spring and summer, and a cool autumn and winter.

Other climate zones exist too, such as mountain climates, which are cold, wet and windy, and desert climates, which are very dry.

3-second sum-up

Climate is the pattern of weather over a long time.

Microclimates

Weather experts say that some places have their own microclimate, or local climate. In cities, the heat coming from buildings makes the climate hotter than in the surrounding countryside. It's cold and windy on mountains, but valleys often have a warmer microclimate because they are sheltered from winds.

Polar zone

Polar zone

Temperate zone

Tropical zone

Temperate zone

Polar zone

Temperate zone

Tropical zone

Earth has three main climate zones: polar, tropical and temperate.

Watery world

A large part of our planet is covered in water. This water lies in the five oceans, and in rivers and lakes around the world. Some is frozen in glaciers and ice sheets. In this chapter, you can discover more about our watery world, from the largest and deepest lakes, to the long journey of rivers from their source to the sea and the amazing landscape that lies under the oceans.

Watery world
Glossary

arch At the coast, when a cave erodes to form an arch of rock.

bacteria The simplest and smallest forms of life. They exist in large numbers in air, water and soil, and in living and dead creatures and plants, and are often a cause of disease.

bay A part of the sea, partly surrounded by a wide curve of the land along the coast.

cirque A round, bowl-shaped hollow area that forms in the side of a mountain.

crater lake A lake that forms in the crater of a volcano that is not active.

current The movement of water in the sea or a river.

delta An area of land made from sediment laid down by rivers, shaped like a triangle, and where a river may split into several smaller rivers before entering the sea.

erode To gradually destroy and remove the surface of something through the action of wind, rain or other natural agents.

estuary The wide part of a river where it flows into the sea.

evaporate When a liquid evaporates, it changes into a gas, for example, water turns into steam.

floodplain An area of flat land beside a river that becomes flooded when there is too much water for the river to hold.

glacier A large mass of ice, formed by snow on mountains, that moves, usually very slowly, down a valley.

gravity The force that attracts objects in space towards each other, and that pulls objects on Earth towards the centre of the planet, so that things fall to the ground when they are dropped.

headland An area of high land that sticks out from the coast into the sea.

magma Very hot liquid rock found below the Earth's crust.

meander A curve in a river.

mineral A substance naturally present in the Earth and not formed from animal or vegetable matter, for example gold and salt.

moraine A mass of soil and rock carried along by a glacier and left when it melts.

mouth (river) The place where a river joins the sea.

oxbow lake A lake that forms when a bend in a river is separated from the river.

rift lake When the movement of the Earth's tectonic plates makes huge blocks of rock rise or fall, a rift lake can form in the hollow.

seamount A mountain under the sea.

sediment Sand, stones, mud and other materials carried by water or wind and left, for example, on the bottom of a lake or river.

snout (glacier) The end of a glacier, where the ice melts.

stack At the coast, when an arch of rock collapses to leave just a column of rock.

tectonic plate One of the huge sheets of rock that form the Earth's surface.

tide The regular rise and fall in the level of the sea, caused by the pull of the Moon and Sun.

trench A deep valley in the ocean floor.

Oceans and seas

...in 30 seconds

Do you know why the Earth is known as the Blue Planet? It's because more than two-thirds of its surface is covered by water. There are five oceans: the Pacific, Atlantic, Indian, Southern and Arctic.

The Pacific Ocean is the largest. It stretches nearly halfway around the globe. It's almost as big as all of the other oceans put together! The Arctic is the smallest. For most of the year, the Arctic Ocean is covered in ice.

A sea is a smaller area of water that forms part of an ocean. For example, the Mediterranean Sea is in the Atlantic Ocean, and the Arabian Sea is in the Indian Ocean. Many seas are at least partly enclosed by land.

About 97 per cent of all the Earth's water lies in the oceans. This water is salty because of the minerals (mostly common salt) dissolved in it. Most of the salt comes from rocks on land, and is washed into the sea by the rain and rivers. Some comes from volcanoes under the sea.

3-second sum-up

Oceans and seas cover more than two-thirds of the Earth.

Ocean currents

The water in the oceans is constantly moving. The wind drives along currents – huge bands of water that flow through the sea like giant rivers. Some carry warm water; others cold.

Currents help to spread heat around the world, and have an important effect on the weather of the places they flow past.

Under the sea

...in 30 seconds

The top layers of the sea are brightly lit by the Sun, but as you dive further down, it quickly gets darker. Below a depth of about 100 m (330 feet), it is pitch black and extremely cold.

A remarkable landscape lies beneath the sea. On the ocean floor, there are vast, flat plains, covered with sediment made from the remains of sea plants and animals. Long chains of mountains, called ocean ridges, form where tectonic plates move apart, allowing magma to rise up.

There are also single mountains, called seamounts, some of which are higher than the highest mountains on land. Trenches are deep valleys in the ocean floor.

Deepest of all is the Mariana Trench in the Pacific. The bottom of this trench is 10,994 m (36,070 feet) below the ocean surface. If Mount Everest, the highest mountain in the world, was placed in the Mariana Trench, it would be covered by 1.6 km (1 mile) of water!

3-second sum-up

Beneath the sea are flat plains, high mountains and deep trenches.

Black smokers

Along some ocean ridges, super-hot, dark-coloured water shoots out of vents (openings) in the seabed. These vents are known as black smokers. Minerals in the water form chimney-like structures around the vents. Groups of animals live around black smokers. The animals include giant tube worms, 2 m (6 feet) long, crabs and shrimps. They live on bacteria that grow using the minerals in the vent water.

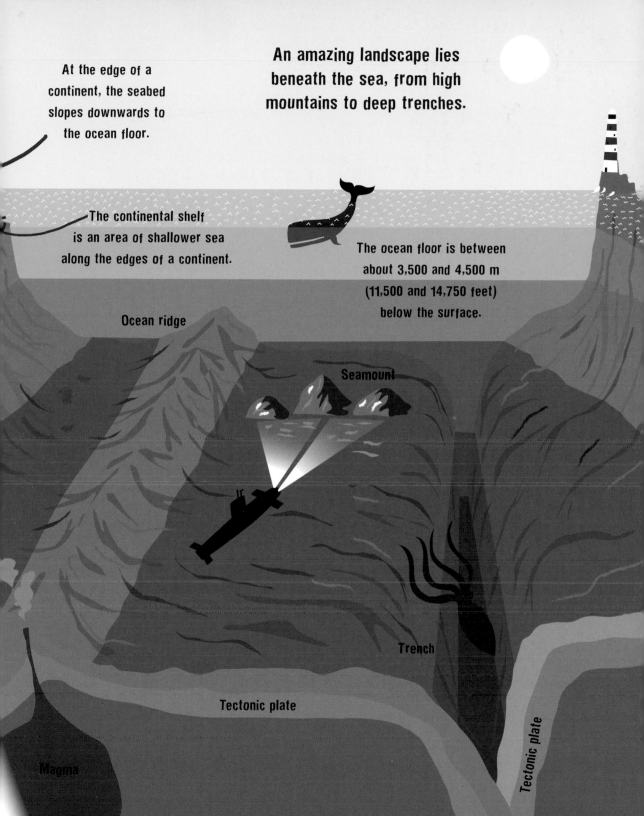

At the edge of a continent, the seabed slopes downwards to the ocean floor.

An amazing landscape lies beneath the sea, from high mountains to deep trenches.

The continental shelf is an area of shallower sea along the edges of a continent.

The ocean floor is between about 3,500 and 4,500 m (11,500 and 14,750 feet) below the surface.

Ocean ridge

Seamount

Trench

Tectonic plate

Tectonic plate

Magma

Coasts

...in 30 seconds

At the coast, the sea meets the land. Here, the powerful forces of the wind and waves erode the rocks. They reshape the landscape, carving out cliffs, caves and arches.

Estuaries are places where rivers meet the sea. The coast bends inland at an estuary. Estuaries have low-lying mud banks that are uncovered at low tide.

In most areas, the sea rises and falls on the shore twice a day with the tides. It's the pull of the Moon's gravity on the Earth that causes tides.

Gravity pulls on the water in the oceans, making the water build up on the side facing the Moon. The water also builds up on the opposite side. These places have high tide. As the Earth spins, places move in and out of the areas pulled by the Moon, so they have low tide and then high tide again.

The Sun also plays a part in the tides. It makes them higher and lower at different times of year.

3-second sum-up

Coasts are where the sea meets the land.

3-minute mission Bending waves

You need: • Large, deep tray • Cup
• Rectangular plastic lid

1 Pour 1 cm (½ inch) of water into the tray.

2 Stand the cup upside down in the middle of the tray.

3 Make small waves in the water with the edge of the lid.

4 The waves will bend around the cup to meet on the other side. This is how waves bend around headlands on coasts.

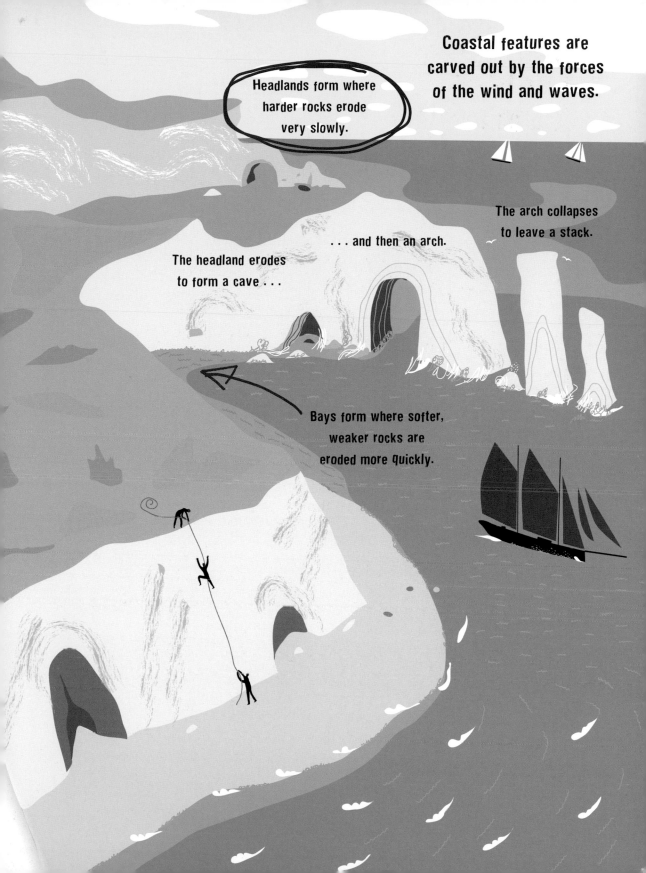

Rivers

...in 30 seconds

Just one per cent of the water on Earth flows in rivers and fills lakes. This is fresh water. Rivers carry water from the land to the sea. On the way, they shape the landscape that they flow through.

As it flows, a river carries along a load of sediments (rock, mud and clay). The rocks wear out the river bed, carving out valleys. Some of this load – mostly the mud and clay – is dumped on the river's floodplain, where it creates rich land ideal for farming.

Near the sea, the river reaches its final stage. It flows into the sea at its mouth. Here, it dumps more sediment, which builds up a fan-shaped area of new land, called a delta.

The Nile is the world's longest river. It flows 6,695 km (4,160 miles) through many different countries in Africa, and has made one of the world's largest deltas.

3-second sum-up

A river carries water from the land to the sea.

3-minute mission Make river sediment

You need: • Large tray • Piece of wood a few centimetres thick • Play sand • Jug of water • An outdoor space (this is messy!)

1 Cover the tray with a layer of sand a few millimetres thick. Raise one end of the tray on the wood.

2 Slowly pour some water onto the raised end of the tray. Watch what happens to the sand.

3 The water carries the sand down the tray and drops it at the other end – just as a river carries sediment.

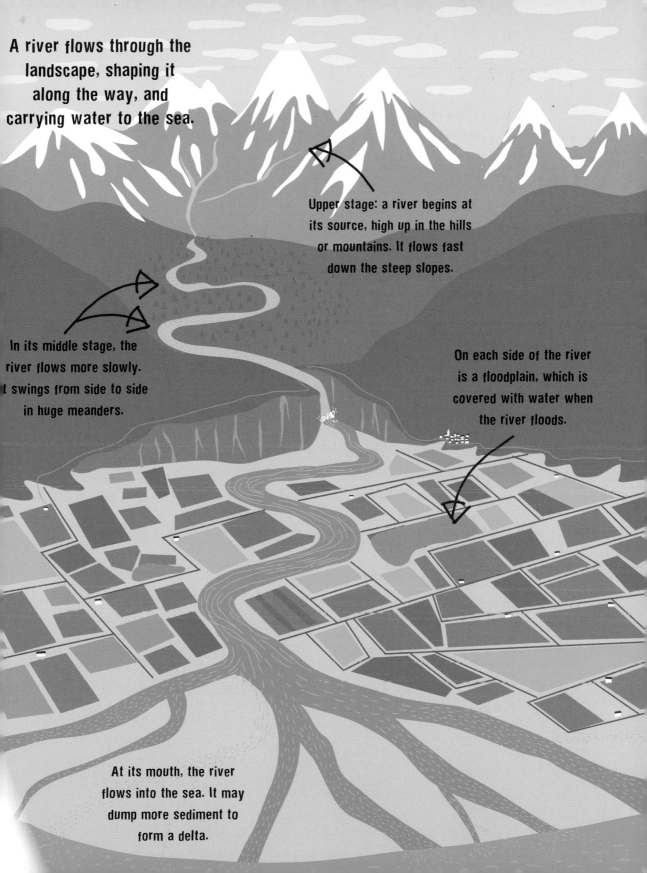

A river flows through the landscape, shaping it along the way, and carrying water to the sea.

Upper stage: a river begins at its source, high up in the hills or mountains. It flows fast down the steep slopes.

In its middle stage, the river flows more slowly. It swings from side to side in huge meanders.

On each side of the river is a floodplain, which is covered with water when the river floods.

At its mouth, the river flows into the sea. It may dump more sediment to form a delta.

Lakes

...in 30 seconds

Take a hollow in the ground and pour in lots of water. You have made a mini lake! That's all a lake is – a hollow filled with water.

There are different kinds of lakes. In mountainous areas, many lakes form in hollows gouged out by ancient glaciers. Oxbow lakes form in river meanders that have been cut off from the river.

When the movement of the Earth's tectonic plates makes huge blocks of rock rise or fall, rift and fault lakes form in the hollows. Crater lakes form in the craters of non-active volcanoes.

How does water reach lakes? Fresh water comes from streams and rivers flowing into them, melted ice from glaciers, or water seeping up from underground. Rainwater falls on them, too.

Some lakes are salty. They form where water dissolves salty minerals from the lake-bed rocks. As the water evaporates, it leaves the salts behind. Large salt-water lakes, such as the Caspian Sea, are called inland seas.

3-second sum-up

A lake is a hollow in the landscape filled with water.

The largest and deepest lakes

The largest lake in the world is Lake Superior, one of North America's Great Lakes. It covers 82,100 sq km (31,700 sq miles) – about the area of 66 million Olympic swimming pools! The deepest lake is Lake Baikal in Russia. Its maximum depth is 1,642 m – that's a mile deep.

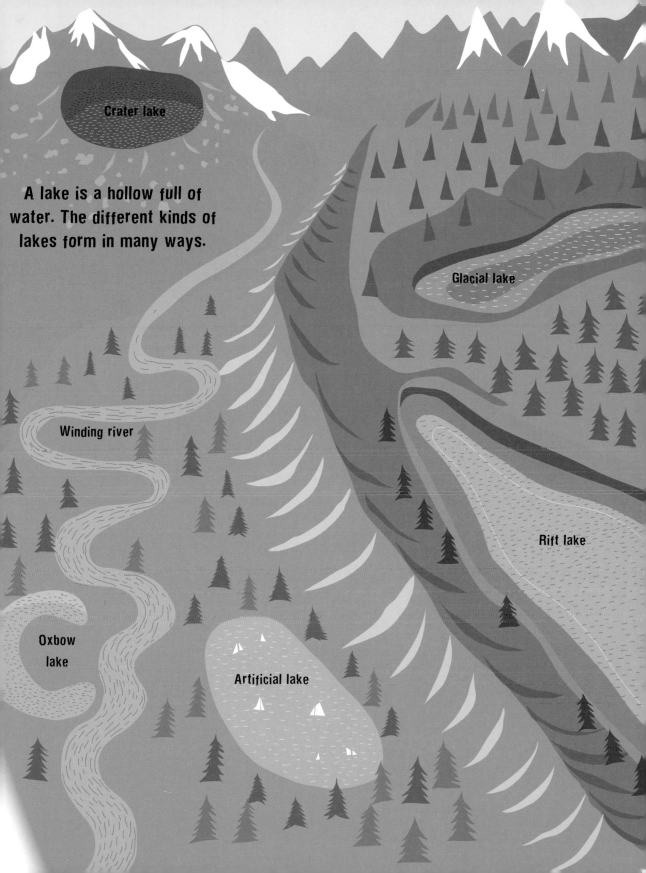

Crater lake

A lake is a hollow full of water. The different kinds of lakes form in many ways.

Glacial lake

Winding river

Rift lake

Oxbow lake

Artificial lake

Glaciers

...in 30 seconds

If you climb to the peaks of the world's highest mountains, you'll see nothing but snow all year round. Gradually, over thousands of years, the deep layers of snow on the mountain tops turn to ice.

They form a great icy river called a glacier, which slides slowly downhill. It's hard to spot a glacier moving. A typical glacier moves along at about 2 m (6 feet) a day.

Glaciers also flow from the ice caps – the enormous, thick sheets of ice that cover Antarctica and Greenland.

Over time, glaciers carve out hollows in mountain slopes, called cirques, and U-shaped valleys with steep sides and flat bottoms.

The end of a glacier is called its snout. Here the ice melts as it arrives, dumping bits of rock that it has carried along.

Many glaciers end in oceans or lakes. Huge chunks of ice break off and crash noisily into the water.

3-second sum-up

A glacier is a slow-moving river of ice.

3-minute mission Glaciers from space

You need: • Computer (or tablet or smartphone) with the Google Earth application

1 Open Google Earth.

2 Key in 'Himalaya mountains' in the 'search' box.

3 Zoom in to see the Himalaya mountains in more detail.

4 Key in 'Mount Everest'. Can you spot the glaciers that flow from its slopes?

Amazing ecosystems

An ecosystem is a community of living things (plants and animals) as well as non-living things (rocks, air and water) that work together and depend on each other to survive. An ecosystem can be as big as a desert or as small as a puddle. In this chapter, you can read about some of the world's great ecosystems, from steamy rainforests to isolated islands, freezing-cold Poles and colourful coral reefs.

Amazing ecosystems
Glossary

axis An imaginary line through the centre of the Earth, around which it turns.

canopy The second to top layer of the rainforest, where the tree tops spread over the forest like a roof.

continent One of the large land masses of the Earth, such as Europe, Asia or Africa.

coral reef Structures in the sea made from rock created by tiny animals found in the water.

ecosystem All the living and non-living things found in a particular area.

emergent layer The top layer of a rainforest, where very tall trees grow above the canopy.

Equator An imaginary line around the Earth at an equal distance from the North and South Poles.

isolation Being in isolation means being separate from everything else.

lowland rainforest A kind of rainforest found around the Equator that has a lot of rainfall. Lowland rainforests are found on low land, up to 1 km (0.6 miles) above sea level.

mammal Any animal that gives birth to live babies and feeds its young on milk. Horses, humans and whales are all mammals.

mangrove rainforest Rainforest that grows in coastal areas in the tropics – the trees can cope with salty water from the sea.

montane rainforest Rainforest that is found in mountain areas.

oasis An area in the desert where there is water and where plants can grow.

Poles The two points at the opposite ends of the Earth's axis.

polyp (coral) A small and very simple sea creature with a body shaped like a tube.

rainforest A thick forest in tropical parts of the world that have a lot of rain.

rain shadow An area that has little rainfall because it is sheltered by hills from the winds that bring rain.

sand dune A hill of sand formed by the wind, near the sea or in a desert.

tropics The area just above and below the Equator. The climate is warm or hot, and moist all year round.

understory In a rainforest, the second layer up from the forest floor – little sunshine reaches this area.

Deserts

...in 30 seconds

Picture a desert and you probably imagine vast areas of scorching hot sand. But not all deserts are sandy. Some are rocky or stony. Antarctica is icy! In sandy deserts, the wind blows the loose sand into gigantic piles, called sand dunes, which can be hundreds of metres high.

All deserts are dry. Some are far inland, where rain rarely falls. Some form along the edges of mountain ranges. Any rain falls on the mountains, not the land alongside.

The Atacama Desert lies in the rain shadow of the Andes Mountains. Parts of it have had no rain for hundreds of years.

Many deserts, such as the Sahara in Africa, are baking hot in the daytime all year round. Some, such as the Gobi in northern Asia, are very cold in the winter. All deserts are cold at night.

Some amazing plants and animals live in these harsh conditions. They have special survival features. Camels can go for days without drinking, and weeks without eating. They turn the fat in their humps into food and save water by producing very dry droppings.

3-second sum-up

A desert is a place where it hardly ever rains.

3-minute mission Blow a dune

You need: • An old tray • Play sand

1 Do this experiment outdoors. Put a handful of sand on the tray and shape it into a model sand dune.

2 With your mouth level with the edge of the tray, blow gently across the dune.

3 Can you see the sand blowing up one side of the dune and down the other?

In a sandy desert, dunes are
shaped by the wind. Some plants
and animals have adapted to live
in the harsh conditions.

Star dune – a
star-shaped dune

Barchan dune
– a crescent-
shaped dune

Acacia tree

Seif dune – a long,
narrow dune

Camels

Transverse dune
– a long dune lying
at right angles to
the wind direction

An oasis is an area of water in
a desert, which usually comes
from water underground.

Monitor
lizard

Sand viper

Rainforests

...in 30 seconds

Rainforests grow in the tropics, on either side of the Equator. The climate is hot and humid, and rain pours down almost every day. More than two-thirds of the world's plant species are found in tropical rainforests.

Rainforests cover about 6 per cent of the Earth's surface. They include lowland rainforests, such as the Amazon; montane rainforests, which grow on mountain slopes; and mangrove forests, which grow along coasts.

The largest is the Amazon rainforest, along the banks of the Amazon River in South America. It's twice the size of India!

There may be hundreds of species of plants and animals living in an area of rainforest the size of a football pitch. The most common animals are insects, but hundreds of birds, primates, reptiles, spiders and frogs live there too.

3-second sum-up

Rainforests are hot and have lots of rain.

Rainforest plants

Rainforest plants contain many useful substances and foods.

- Latex, the sap of the rubber tree, and the raw material for making rubber. The rubber is used to make tyres.

- Foods such as Brazil nuts, cashew nuts, coffee, mangos and bananas.

- Bamboo and rattan, used for making furniture.

- The ingredients for some of our favourite treats – cocoa for making chocolate, and vanilla for ice cream.

Poles

...in 30 seconds

Go to the very ends of the Earth and you'll find the Poles. They are at either end of the Earth's axis – an imaginary line running through the Earth from north to south.

At the North and South Poles, it is icy and bitterly cold. The North Pole lies in the middle of the Arctic Ocean, which is frozen all year round. The area of ice grows in winter and shrinks in summer. The South Pole is in Antarctica, a huge continent covered with a thick sheet of ice.

The Poles are cold all year round, but extremely cold in winter. In Antarctica, temperatures can fall as low as -60°C (-76°F). The Sun never rises in the middle of winter, but never sets in the middle of the short summer.

Animals such as polar bears, penguins and seals have adapted to life in the freezing polar conditions. They fend off the cold with thick layers of fur, feathers or fat.

3-second sum-up

At the North and South Poles, it is cold all the time.

3-minute mission Floating iceberg

You need: • Drinking glass • Ice cube • Ruler

1 Half-fill the glass with water. Drop in an ice cube to make a model iceberg.

2 Very slowly add water until the glass is full to the brim.

3 Using your ruler, estimate how many millimetres of your iceberg is above the surface and how much is below.

4 You should find that there is about nine times as much under the water as above.

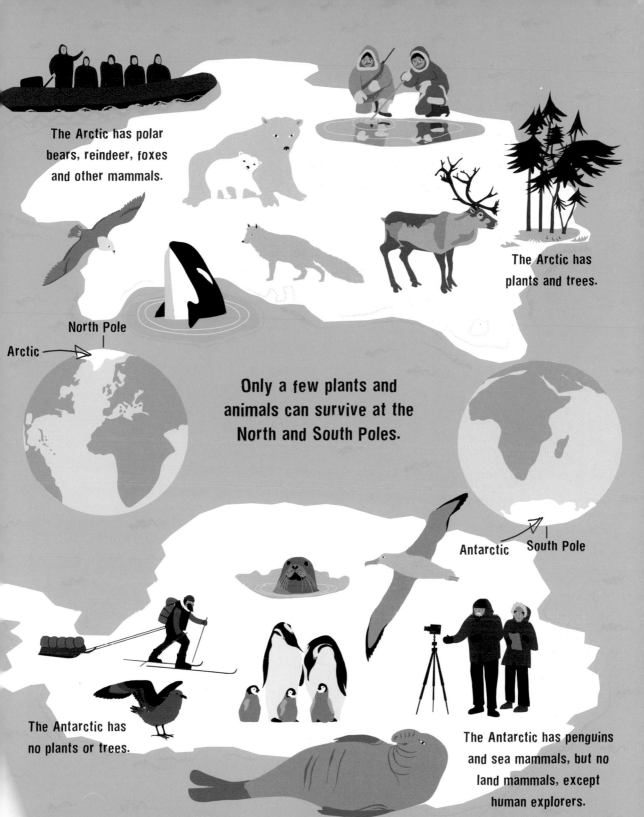

The Arctic has polar bears, reindeer, foxes and other mammals.

The Arctic has plants and trees.

North Pole

Arctic

Only a few plants and animals can survive at the North and South Poles.

Antarctic South Pole

The Antarctic has no plants or trees.

The Antarctic has penguins and sea mammals, but no land mammals, except human explorers.

Islands

...in 30 seconds

An island is a piece of land surrounded on all sides by sea.
Islands range from tiny coral islands just a few metres wide to
enormous continental islands hundreds of kilometres across.
Some islands are low-lying; others have high mountains.

**Islands have a wide variety of climates, from hot and wet in the
tropics, to cold and wet towards the Poles. They are often windy
places, with no shelter from winds blowing across the sea.**

Greenland is the world's biggest island. Three-quarters
of the island is covered in a thick ice sheet. It is warmer
around the coast, and this is where most people live.

Many islands are home to plants and animals that are not found in any
other part of the world. Because of the islands' isolation, their wildlife
has evolved differently. The Galapagos islands lie off the west coast of
South America. They are home to giant tortoises 1.5 m (5 feet) long!
They have evolved long necks for feeding on tall plants.

3-second sum-up

An island is
a piece
of land
surrounded
by water.

3-minute mission Floating seeds

If seeds float to an island, they may grow into plants there.

You need: • Large bowl • Seeds or fruit, such as dried beans
and peas, apple, brazil nut, sunflower seeds

Think about whether each seed or fruit will float or sink. Test
each one. Let the seeds float in water for as long as possible,
to see if they might reach land without sinking.

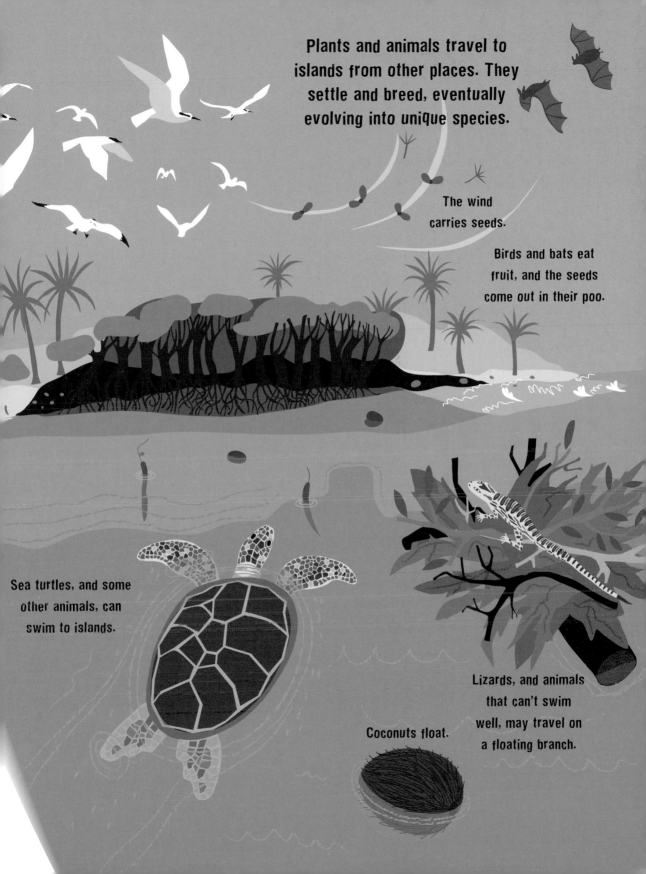

Plants and animals travel to islands from other places. They settle and breed, eventually evolving into unique species.

The wind carries seeds.

Birds and bats eat fruit, and the seeds come out in their poo.

Sea turtles, and some other animals, can swim to islands.

Lizards, and animals that can't swim well, may travel on a floating branch.

Coconuts float.

Coral reefs

...in 30 seconds

Brightly coloured fish dart through clear, sparkling water, among coral shaped like trees, fans and even brains. Welcome to the coral reef!

Reefs are home to a huge variety of animals, including two-thirds of all ocean fish, sponges, starfish and crabs.

Coral is living material, made up of thousands of tiny animals, called polyps. The polyps have soft bodies, protected by hard, chalky cases that they build around themselves. When a polyp dies, its body rots away, but its hard case is left behind.

New polyps grow on top of the old cases, and, over many years, the cases build up into different shapes, with living coral on the outside. Over hundreds and thousands of years, groups of coral join together to form long reefs.

Coral mostly grows in warm, shallow water. This is why coral reefs are mostly found in the tropics – along coasts and around the tops of underwater mountains.

The Great Barrier Reef in Australia is the world's largest coral reef. It covers about 35 million hectares (86 million acres) – the size of 70 million football fields!

3-second sum-up

Coral reefs are built by living animals.

3-minute mission The Great Barrier Reef

You need: • Computer (or tablet or smartphone) with the Google Earth application

1 Start up Google Earth.

2 Find Australia and navigate to the north-east coast.

3 Can you see the Great Barrier Reef along the coast?

Future Earth

What will Planet Earth be like in the future? Nobody knows, of course. One thing is certain – it is changing at a very fast rate. All over the world, the weather is getting wilder and precious ecosystems are being destroyed. Many of these changes are down to human activities, but it's not all bad news. In this chapter, you can find out more about what is happening and about what can be done to help to save the Earth.

Future Earth
Glossary

atmosphere The mixture of gases that surrounds the Earth.

carbon dioxide A gas breathed out by people and animals and also produced by burning carbon.

climate The regular pattern of weather conditions of a place.

coral reef Structures in the sea made from rock created by tiny animals found in the water.

drought A long period of time when there is little or no rain.

ecosystem All the living and non-living things found in a particular area.

erode To gradually destroy and remove the surface of something through the action of wind, rain or other natural agents.

extinct When a plant or animal no longer exists because it has died out.

global warming The problem of the rise in temperature of the Earth's atmosphere, which is caused by the increase of particular gases, especially carbon dioxide, including those produced by human activity.

greenhouse effect The gradual rise in the temperature of the Earth's atmosphere, caused by naturally occurring gases, such as carbon dioxide, which trap the heat of the Sun.

landfill An area of land where waste material is buried under the Earth's surface.

pollute To add dirty or harmful substances to land, air or water so that it is no longer pleasant or safe to use.

rainforest A thick forest in tropical parts of the world that have a lot of rain.

recycle To treat things that have already been used so that they can be used again.

resource A supply of something that a country or people can use.

solar power Turning energy from the Sun's rays into energy that people can use.

species A group of animals or plants that are similar and able to breed with each other.

thermostat A device that measures and controls the temperature of a machine or room, by switching the heating or cooling system on and off as needed.

wind power Turning the energy of the wind into useful energy that people can use.

Changing climate

...in 30 seconds

Did you know that the climate changes over time?
Scientists believe that today's climate may be changing faster than at any time in the last 10,000 years.

The climate can change naturally. But most experts agree that today's changes are happening faster because of human activities.

To understand how, we need to head off into the atmosphere. Some of the gases in the Earth's atmosphere trap heat from the Sun. This is called the greenhouse effect, and it keeps our planet warm. The gas that traps most heat is carbon dioxide.

Every day, human activities, such as burning coal, oil and gas, give off carbon dioxide. The carbon dioxide rises into the atmosphere. It traps heat, making the Earth warmer. Scientists call this global warming. The changing climate is making the weather wilder. We're seeing more storms, floods and droughts.

We can help reduce global warming by using less fuel for energy and transport and by developing fuels that produce less carbon dioxide. Trees absorb carbon dioxide, so cutting down fewer trees and planting new trees are ways to help our planet.

3-second sum-up

Climate change is a change in weather patterns.

Cutting energy costs

It is easy to cut down energy costs at home. Your thermostat should be set to the lowest comfortable temperature – between 18 and 21°C (64–70°F). If a family turns down the thermostat by just one degree, it will save £65 (US $100) a year. And the household will have saved 260 kg (573 lb) of the greenhouse-gas carbon dioxide from going into the atmosphere.

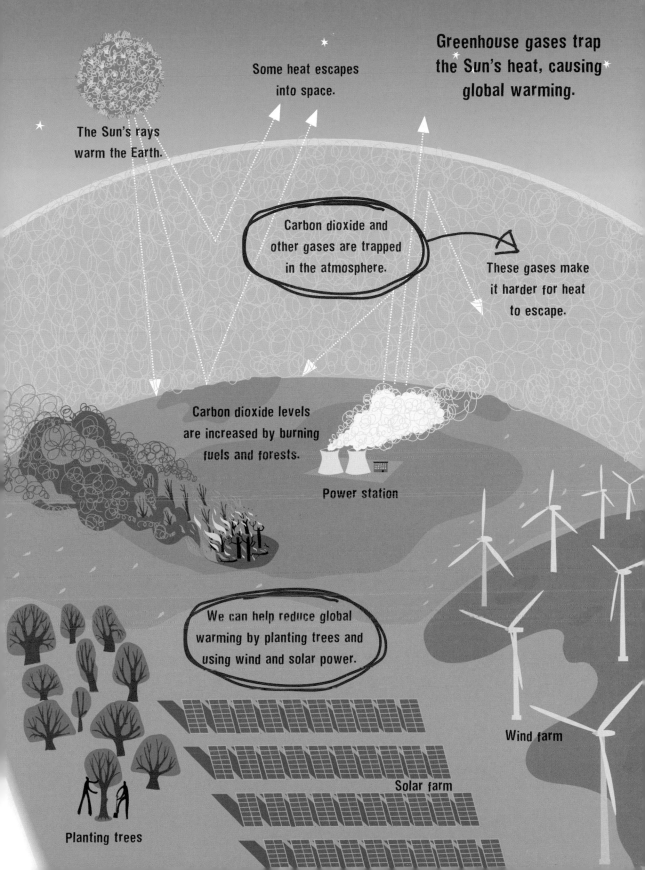

The Sun's rays warm the Earth.

Some heat escapes into space.

Greenhouse gases trap the Sun's heat, causing global warming.

Carbon dioxide and other gases are trapped in the atmosphere.

These gases make it harder for heat to escape.

Carbon dioxide levels are increased by burning fuels and forests.

Power station

We can help reduce global warming by planting trees and using wind and solar power.

Wind farm

Solar farm

Planting trees

Fighting waste

...in 30 seconds

Every year, we use about 500 billion plastic bags. That's about 70 for each person – and most of them are thrown away! We also throw away a huge amount of plastic bottles, tin cans and paper.

Most waste is burnt or buried in the ground. This buried rubbish is called landfill. Some of it will take thousands of years to rot away, and we're quickly running out of suitable places for landfill sites.

But much of our waste can be reused or recycled, so that we use fewer resources and create less rubbish. We can often reuse plastic bottles before recycling them.

If we recycle our cans, it saves energy. Making aluminium cans from old ones uses up only one-twentieth of the energy needed to make new ones. A plastic bag made from recycled polythene uses one-eighth of the amount of water needed to make a new one. We can also help to fight waste by buying recycled products.

3-second sum-up

Our waste pollutes the environment.

3-minute mission Make a plant container

You need: • Clean 2-litre plastic bottle • Handful of gravel • Potting compost • A few plant seeds • Scissors • An adult helper

1 Ask an adult to cut around the bottle about one-third up from the base.

2 Put a 2-cm (1-in) layer of gravel in the base. Cover with 5 cm (2 in) of compost.

3 Push in the seeds and water them.

4 Make four vertical 2-cm (1-in) cuts in the top rim of the base. Push the top of the bottle over the base.

5 Put the plant container on a sunny windowsill.

Watch the seeds grow!

Waste materials like paper, glass, plastic and cans, can all be recycled to make new products.

Toy

Shoes

T-shirt

Juice drink carton

Wrapping paper

Puzzle pieces

Earrings

Bottles

Material for road surfacing

Marbles

Car parts

Chair

Umbrella

Paper

Glass

Plastic

Cans

Vanishing habitats

...in 30 seconds

All over the world, humans are destroying wildlife habitats, putting plants and animals in danger. People clear habitats to make space for new homes, factories and farmland. They pollute the water in our rivers and along our coasts.

When a habitat is destroyed, plants and animals have to adapt to the new conditions or find somewhere else to live. If they cannot, they may die out.

Rainforest habitats are at great risk. Every second, the world loses a patch of rainforest the size of a football pitch. People chop down trees for their wood, and to clear space for mines and farms. Hundreds of species of rainforest plants and animals are wiped out, and the lives of rainforest people are destroyed too.

Pollution, mining and the collecting of rare corals and shells threaten coral reefs. About a quarter of reefs have already been destroyed, and another 60 per cent are at serious risk.

3-second sum-up

Many habitats around the world are being destroyed.

3-minute mission Extinct or under threat?

Many species of plants and animals have already become extinct, and many more are on the brink of dying out. Look up the animals listed. Are they extinct, or under threat? What is their habitat and what is happening to it?

Species:
Orangutan
Sumatran rhino
Sun bear
Black spider monkey
Tree kangaroo

Cutting down rainforests destroys unique habitats and erodes the land.

Trees are cut or burnt down to clear the land.

Farmers use the land for a while to grow crops.

Growing crops uses up the nutrients in the soil, so the farmers leave the land and farm elsewhere.

The land is eroded and nothing grows.

Saving the Earth

...in 30 seconds

Here are some ideas for things YOU can do to help to save the Earth.

- Join an eco-club at school or gather some friends to start one up. Decide on your campaign. Can you persuade people to cut energy or water use around the school?

- Talk to your friends and family about saving fuel by walking, cycling or taking the bus for some journeys instead of travelling by car.

- Remember to switch off the lights when you leave the room and spend a minute less in the shower. You'll save money as well as precious energy!

- Reuse as many items at home as possible. Plastic bottles, cardboard and scrap paper are handy for all kinds of craft activities. Make sure the materials no one can use any more go in the recycling box.

- Join with some friends to raise some money for an eco-project, for example, saving a threatened habitat.

3-second sum-up

You can help to save the planet in many ways.

The Three Rs

Remember to focus on the three Rs – that's Reduce, Reuse and Recycle.

Reduce: see if you can walk more often, rather than travelling by car.

Reuse: take your old clothes and toys to a charity shop.

Recycle: take glass bottles, paper and tins to a recycling bank.

Some of the small things we can do to help make a big difference and save our Earth.

Using the bus

Planting trees

SAVE OUR EARTH

Campaigning

Going to the charity shop.

Cycling

Walking

Having a quicker shower

Picking up litter

Using the bottle bank

Discover more

FICTION BOOKS

Attack of the Shidas: AKAs Save Planet Earth! by Muthoni Muchemi, Kindle Edition **(Storymoja and Worldreader, 2012)**

Stories For a Fragile Planet by Kenneth Steven **(Lion Children's Books, 2012)**

NON-FICTION BOOKS

Discover Science: Planet Earth by Barbara Taylor and Deborah Chancellor **(Kingfisher, 2011)**

Encyclopedia of Planet Earth by Anna Claybourne and Gill Doherty **(Usborne Publishing Ltd, 2013)**

Explorers: Planet Earth by Daniel Gilpin and Peter Bull **(Kingfisher Books Ltd, 2014)**

Horrible Geography of the World by Anita Ganeri **(Scholastic, 2010)**

How the World Works: A Hands-on Guide to Our Amazing Planet by Christiane Dorion **(Candlewick Press, 2010)**

Planet Earth by Katie Daynes **(Usborne Publishing Ltd, 2008)**

Planet Earth! A Kids Book About Planet Earth by Alexander G. Michaels **(Kindle Edition, 2013)**

Planet Earth – The World in Infographics by Jon Richards and Ed Simkins **(Wayland, 2013)**

Story of Planet Earth by Abigail Wheatley **(Usborne Publishing Ltd, 2013)**

Why Does Earth Spin?: And Other Questions about Our Planet by Mary Kay Carson **(Sterling, 2014)**

DVDs – suitable for all ages

Frozen Planet – The Complete Series by David Attenborough (2entertain, 2011)

Inside Planet Earth (Demand DVD, 2013)

Planet Earth: The Complete Series by David Attenborough (2entertain, 2010)

WEBSITES

An Ecological System
http://www.geography4kids.com/files/land_ecosystem.html
All about ecosystems

The Earth's structure
http://www.bbc.co.uk/schools/gcsebitesize/science/ocr_gateway_pre_2011/rocks_metals/3_does_the_earth_move1.shtml
Earth's structure, plate tectonics, rocks

Information and Facts about Rivers
http://primaryhomeworkhelp.co.uk/rivers.html
Features of rivers, flooding, pollution

National Geographic – Climate and Weather
http://www.watchknowlearn.org/Video.aspx?VideoID=3929&CategoryID=2671
Video about the differences between climate and weather

Planets for Kids
http://www.planetsforkids.org/planet-earth.html
The planets in our solar system

What is happening in the ocean?
http://climatekids.nasa.gov/ocean/
About oceans and climate

Weather and climate
http://climatekids.nasa.gov/menu/weather-and-climate/
Pages on all aspects of climate change

Index